WM Resources Ltd presents

The Simple Guide to Freelancing

Branding yourself for Success

By Wolfgang Matejek

Copyright Notice

Copyright © 2016 by WM Resources Ltd.

All rights reserved. This book or any portion thereof may not be reproduced or used in any manner whatsoever without the express written permission of the publisher except for the use of brief quotations in a book review.

Printed in the United States of America
First Edition, 2016

ISBN-13: 978-1535555746
ISBN-10: 1535555742

http://www.wmresourcesltd.com

Contents

COPYRIGHT NOTICE ....

INTRODUCTION 1

FREELANCING – WHAT THE HECK IS THAT? 3

YOU ARE YOUR OWN BRAND..5

SETTING YOURSELF UP AS A BRAND 7

DEFINING YOUR VALUES AND BRAND VISION 10

LET'S BUILD YOUR BRAND..13

    Your "Visual" Brand Image..13
    Your "Invisible" Brand Image (Perception)..........................17

WHERE CAN YOU FIND WORK..20

HOW TO ENHANCE YOUR BRAND AWARENESS....................................23

    Social Networks..24
    Blogging 27
    Personal Relationships & Associations 30
    Online Advertising 30

NOW THAT ALL THE TECHNICAL BUSINESS STUFF HAS BEEN DEALT WITH - LET'S FOCUS ON RUNNING YOUR FREELANCE BUSINESS! 33

HOW TO & HOW MUCH TO CHARGE FOR YOUR SERVICES 34

LEGAL STUFF – TERMS & CONDITIONS, PRIVACY POLICY ETC.................40

INVOICING FOR YOUR SERVICES 43

CLIENTS – YOUR DAILY BREAD & BUTTER..45

    Always deliver outstanding work 47
    Exceeding expectations 49
    Other things to do to keep in good stead with your clients.52
    Things which surely will kill your client relationship............53

RESOURCES **56**
- *Freelancer Portals* *56*
- *Accounting Software* *58*
- *Free Office Software* *58*
- *Social Networks* *59*
- *Domain Name & Hosting Services* *59*

OTHER BOOKS BY THE AUTHOR **60**

Introduction

With the job market uncertainty as it is, there may be a compelling reason for you to work as a freelancer. This in itself offers a two-way prong of opportunities based on your skills and knowledge.

For one, you can earn extra income with freelancing, utilising your existing skills and knowledge in your spare time. Secondly, the skills and experience you use during your freelancing period will also add to your skills portfolio, giving you more opportunities to carve out your desired niche of where you may wish to start your own business career in the future.

While this all sounds quite simple, there are potential hurdles you may face. While I am not able to tell you what these may be, since everyone's approach to becoming a freelancer may be different, I can however tell you that whatever those hurdles may be, you will need to overcome them one way or another.

I myself started my career in the corporate world, before deciding to become a freelancer in the world of bespoke IT CRM systems training and personal development. The major hurdle I faced was the drop into the unknown. I was facing the situation of where do I find paying clients for my services, or working potentially for people I have never met, and establishing myself as an expert in my field among others.

My perseverance though paid off and I landed my first big contract with an international corporation, which not only was very exciting to work for, but in addition paid very handsomely for the work I delivered.

I haven't looked back since, as more contracts for some very well known brands came through and kept me busy all over the world. To see what I do, or if you wish to hire me for your training projects, you are invited to visit my website at http://www.wmresourcesltd.com.

With my 'Simple Guide to Freelancing' I am going to share with you a lot of what I have learned over the years.

Let's get started...

Freelancing –
What the heck is that?

Google the term "freelancing" and you will find the Wikipedia definition of a Freelancer as:

"A freelancer or freelance worker is a term commonly used for a person who is self-employed and is not necessarily committed to a particular employer long-term."

In essence this means that you will be working for someone without actually being an employee and not receiving any benefits associated with being a full-time member of staff.

Freelancers, while not being on a company's payroll, can charge for their work by the hour, days or job. As a freelancer you are actually a one-person business, which depending on where in the world you are, may place different meanings and conditions on your role.

This may include different values on how much you can charge or taxes you may have to pay. Some countries can vary in this quite a bit more than others.

One thing though that is the same no matter where you are in the world, is the fact that the work and skills you provide must be better than the employees already working in the company. Clients will not accept any lack of skills or sloppy work from any freelancer and your acquired contract may be short-lived if you fail to deliver in this.

No matter what services you provide, you must always aim to stand out against the average employee.

Since you are a one-man band, a superb one-man show at that, your skills are your bread and butter. But in addition to your client facing skills, you will also need additional skills to keep your freelancing business alive. The skills include but are not limited to:

- *General marketing skills to promote yourself and your services;*
- *Networking skills to attract new clients;*
- *Basic accounting skills in order to prepare your own invoicing and managing your expenses*

You are your own BRAND

What is branding? This can be virtually anything such as a particular image, sound, flavour, smell or a person... well, anything or everything really.

Many books have been written on the subject of branding, mainly geared towards large businesses and corporate. In any case you will already have seen or heard of brands in many guises such as:

- *The golden arch of McDonalds*
- *The fruit symbol of Apple*
- *The sound of a Coca Cola bottle being opened*
- *The sound your pc makes when starting Windows*
- *"Vorsprung durch Technik" phrase for Audi cars*
- *... Plus countless others.*

As any business knows, branding is very important to stand out from the competition. And in this modern world, branding is not only reserved for large corporations but also small businesses and even freelancers.

You must separate yourself from your competition and appear to be more appealing to your target market by creating your own personal brand.

While you may not immediately have a stylish logo to be associated with you and your services, having a catchy/good branding or tagline phrase will set you off to a good start.

In a fierce market it is no longer a choice to stand out from the crowd, it's an absolute **MUST**!

Setting yourself up as a Brand

To be easily identified by future clients, they need to know who you are and what you have to offer. Setting yourself up as a brand is the way to go. You can choose to make this a simple or more complicated affair. It's entirely your choice, but it's worth remembering that whichever you choose, this will be the way your clients will identify you.

Along the branding route should also be a logo. Great logo designers can be found on Fiverr.com. Once you have the logo in place, you will need to also have a website to spread your message. Freelancers without a website just do not get the exposure they need to attract prospective clients.

While the actual website design can be outsourced quite cheaply if need be, you will have to register your website domain name first. My preferred website domain registrar is GoDaddy.com and for hosting I recommend to go with Hostgator.com.

Even though GoDaddy.com also offers hosting, their prices are somewhat higher than the offerings from Hostgator.com. The choice of course is yours, but I would advise you to compare both side by side.

Here are some tips on choosing your domain name:

- *Keep it simple, not confusing and long!*
- *Choose one that stands out, but keep it clean and professional*
- *Easy to spell and to remember*
- *One that can be associated with your service activity*

Once you have your domain name, it's time to think about the meaty content for your website. While this can be as big as you want it to be, there are four tabs that should definitely be included:

1. *An introduction about who you are with a brief description of your expertise and if you do have some testimonials, include those too.*
2. *A description of the services you offer/provide.*
3. *A portfolio of previous work if you have it. If you don't, then start collecting those pieces of information and add them later.*
4. *And don't forget to add your Contact details!*

Always remember that with everything you do from this point forward, you are now <u>a business</u>! So it is vitally important to always be extremely professional and have everything matching the high quality standards your clients come to expect of you.

If you find that there is anything you don't think you can deliver at a high quality standard, you may have to consider hiring someone else to do it for you instead of letting your standards slip.

To find other freelancers to whom you may wish to outsource some of the work, check out the Resources section at the end of this book. There you will find more than 40 website links to freelancer sites where you could place an ad for your required support.

Defining your Values and Brand Vision

Your branding helps you to stand out of the crowd, making you unique in the way your clients and others will see you. Your brand should be consistent with your personal and professional values.

Your Values describe who you are as a person.

They can depend on many things, such as the environment you came from, the level of education you attained, the people you most admire or aspire to and much more.
But your values can also determine which actions (good or bad) you take, thoughts you may have about various issues (good or bad) and/or even decisions (good or bad) you make.

Some people may regard family as their most important value, for others it may be their friends or their career.

It's important for you to understand that when making decisions of any kind it's always wise to take your personal values into consideration to help you to make the best decision or to find answers. This approach will give you the best balanced solution between being the right decision and within your values.

While building your value proposition always consider what your most important values are and include them in your brand. This will highlight to potential clients and others what your brand is all about and at the same time shows the values you have as a true and individual person.

Your brand vision has your values at its core.

If your brand vision meets your personal values, it shows that you are truly motivated and focused on your brand. You stand behind everything you say.

But in order to reach this point, you may have to first create a clear picture of what it is you want to achieve. Maybe take into account some ideas around things like:

- *What am I passionate about?*
- *Which niche do I want to be in – in terms of personal & professional fulfilment*
- *What can I learn from others, friends, family, mentors etc?*
- *What obstacles did others in my situation have to deal with?*

Answers to these questions may help you to define what you want and how to get there; thereby avoiding, escaping or even improving on previous mistakes and/or errors you may have made.

Let's build your brand

Since your brand is created to establish your trustworthiness and recognisable image to your clients, there are a few key components you should have to create your brand:

Your "Visual" Brand Image

The first impressions of your brand image are the key to your success. This image must look clean, professional, appealing and attractive as can be. In order to achieve this visual brand image there are 5 highly important visions of your image:

1. **Your Website** – will display your business to the largest business market in the world… the internet. It's imperative that you have a fully functional website that introduces your brand, your services and gives information of how you can solve problems for your clients. It will become the largest marketing brochure for you and should be kept up-to-date with new and valid content at all times.

   And with websites being so easy to maintain in

WordPress, there is no reason for you not to show pictures of work you have done, images of people you have worked with (*ask for their permission first though*) or even videos about what you do, etc.

2. **Social Networking** – It goes without saying how important these social networks have become. But just because they are available, be selective of which ones you will sign up to. Once again they do require a certain amount of interaction from you on a regular daily or even weekly or monthly basis.

3. **Images, Photos, Graphics** – Why not include pictures of yourself, your team members, work you have done or projects you have worked on. Include images wherever you can, as long as they make sense and are in relation to the subject matter.
But do avoid anything that could be perceived as giving a bad image, such as pictures throwing up while at a party, silly pictures or pictures others may find offensive.

For the most part treat pictures and photos the same way as the rest of your website and brand image – clean and professional.

4. **Business Cards** – While many feel the way to go is hi-tech, I prefer them still to expand my potential

contacts. They are easy to carry around and easy to hand over to a potential client I just met.

Yes, I am aware that many of them may end up in a bin or the back of the drawer, but they are still a kind and polite way to say 'Let's stay in touch' or 'Let's chat some more over the next few days.
Even with your business card it is important that you pay attention to the style and quality of your business card.

One supplier which comes to mind for having professional business cards printed may be VistaPrint.com.

Make it a keeper by being creative, original and above all unique to stand out from the crowd.

5. **Your e-Mail Signature** – Firstly let me tell you that free email account providers such as Hotmail, AOL, Google etc. are a definite NoNo for business! It may just be me, but any business I come across which uses one of those free email accounts, I usually pass by without any second glance. Businesses which do not feel that it is important to have a professional email address, just doesn't come across as trustworthy.

Once you have your own website domain and hosting account set up, you will also be able to set up a selection of email addresses as part of your domain name. With some hosts offering as many as up to 999 of them...

This means that even as a one-man business, you can have different email addresses such as enquiries@mysite.com, accountsdept@mysite.com, whatever@mysite.com, etc.

Now, back to your email signature...
One way you will communicate with your clients is via email. But not just the email message content is important, but also your signature.

Treat it like your business card. Be creative, original and above all unique to stand out from the crowd and also include your logo or tagline (*if you have one*).

Your "Invisible" Brand Image (Perception)

To create a successful brand it requires more than just the physical image as described in the previous section. There are additional 'invisible' components you need to consider for your brand to be credible and as unique as possible. Here is a selection of ideas for you to mull over:

1. **Is my brand Worth Remembering**? - To get the business you need, your brand and you will have to be noticed and remembered. This sounds easier than it is initially. Here I don't mean to make an impact by being silly or acting weird, but rather doing something in your professional capacity which will leave a positive and memorable impression with your potential clients or contacts.

   Once you are in your role, be passionate about what you do and go the extra mile to show that you are the best person for the job. This doesn't mean though working 15 hours and only billing for 8; that's just being stupid.

2. **Be an Original** – This may be somewhat related to the previous point. By being original, your brand may be perceived as being 'inventive' or even 'groundbreaking' in the approach taken during a project or assignment. This in itself is worth

remembering and must be a good thing. Another way to assess and create originality for your own brand is by reviewing your competitors.

Whatever they are doing poorly or their clients complain about is your trump card to be better than them. If you can identify their shortcomings and apply them to your brand, it not only makes you original but allows you to market yourself as someone who can solve clients problems others fail to solve.

3. **Express Yourself** – Yes, I know it was a Madonna song... Yet here I am talking about you being expressive when talking about your brand. Always keep it real, truthful and meaningful. Do apply this to every level of interaction you may have both professional and/or personal.

   If you master this personal expression part, any potential clients will be enthused by your passion, whereas if you fail to be passionate when talking about your business, you will lose opportunities faster than you can run.

4. **Always Maintain Consistency** – By coming across as a professional you want to ensure that you are always consistent in your work and operate at optimum level. If you always deliver with a

consistent quality, clients will build a relationship with you and remember that you are the go-to person they want to work with. A badly done job will always be remembered and you may never work for that client ever again.

5. **Always be Credible** – The combination of all previous headings is what describes your credibility. To grow your credibility you can also associate yourself with other already established brands. This will help to spread the word among other clients who will hear about you and the work you do.

Try spending time in developing your contacts and aim to display your brand in the various marketing platforms available to you, such as newspapers, radio, magazine interviews, etc.

Where can you find work

Even though I cannot assure you that my tips will work, I want to share with you several ways where you can try to find work:

1. **Use your existing network** – Check out the contacts you already have, such as previous employers, friends, just about anyone you've ever had contact or dealing with. Make sure that everyone knows that you are now a freelancer and available for paid project work assignments.

2. **Publicise your profile & curriculum** – using free online portals such as Freelancer.com or eLance.com to name just two of the most popular ones, gives you a great exposure to the world of project assignments just about anywhere in the world. By using online freelancer portals, you no longer just have to work in your own area of residence, but your clients could also be based anywhere.

   While this may be attractive on the surface, you have to realize that you are in with a stiff competition and very competitive pricing strategies.

I would not attempt building my business solely on working exclusively for clients on those sites, but rather use them to fill gaps in my diary as well as building my reputation and network. Using freelancer sites can be a great way to initially starting to grow your fledgling business venture quite easily and quickly.

3. **Lastly there is the option of advertising** - This allows you the option to placing ads either online or offline or both. The online advertising option gives you a wider exposure, whereby the offline option will target more of your local market area.

Either way, you should ensure that your advert does link back to your live and functioning website, to give viewers of your advert the opportunity to learn more about you and your service offerings.

To get your website to do most of the online marketing for you, it's vital that your site meets important Search Engine Optimisation (SEO) standards.

This will ensure that Google & other search engines will find and list your site in the most favourable search results position.

If you don't know how to do this, one again there are other freelancers who can assist you in this undertaking. Check out Fiverr.com, eLance.com or Freelancer.com for more info.

How to enhance your Brand Awareness

Now that you have your website in place, possibly a FaceBook page as well, it's time to reach out to a larger audience to grow your followers. But we don't want just about anyone to be a follower; we want to be more targeted towards potential clients.

This raises the question of 'How do I increase my brand exposure?', even if you already have some clients, but more importantly if you have none as yet.

Sitting still and waiting for potential clients to 'discover' you just isn't going to work efficiently enough; you will have to 'hunt' them down. So, where do you go to increase your audience?

Social Networks

You cannot dismiss them in any way. It is today one of the best ways to raise brand awareness both for corporate and individual businesses alike. The URL of the social network community you join usually has your username as part of the URL linking to your personal member page.

While it may not be easy to secure the perfect username (*since 1000's of others before you may have already gotten there first*), always try to get as close to your brand, service or even your own name as possible.

Nowadays there are countless social networks out there you can potentially join for free. Some are better than others, but 4 major players do stand out for me:

1. **Twitter.com** – You must by now have heard or even seen tweets from almost every famous person in the world. The messages which give your brand the required exposure are called Tweets. It's very similar to how FaceBook works, but with Tweets you are limited to a maximum of 120 characters in your message.

   To learn what to tweet about, read some of the major brands tweets, as they tend to use Twitter more professionally than some individuals who seem to keep tweeting about the most ridiculous things like... *'just left home... on way to supermarket for weekly shopping... Toby just puked over the backseat...'* and other rubbish like that.

   One other important aspect of your tweets will be that if you keep your tweet short and snappy you can use the left-over characters to include links to your website too. And if you want to share something visual, you can even attach an image.

2. **Facebook.com** – Who hasn't heard of this one...? While it is one of the most famous social networks around, many (*including myself*) do not regard it as a professional network. Even though, it can be utilised to post message about news on your project work, share funny stories or pictures or even to start conversations with likeminded people.

I would say that it's worth checking it out, but it doesn't mean that you have to use it as much as Twitter or Linkedin.com which follows next.

3. **LinkedIn.com** – This really is the all-singing-and-dancing, the bells & whistles of the professional social networks. It is also the world's largest and most recognised professional social networking brand.

   LinkedIn.com allows you to build your brand, associate it with you as an individual and all the people you may have had contact with. Another great option is that previous contacts and/or clients can give feedback on your services and skills and thereby recommend you to new potential clients and enquirers.

   Just search yourself for some people you may have worked with in the past and see who their connections/contacts are, reviews they may have had and anything else they may have shared on their profile.

   Without a doubt, you **MUST** as a freelancer, become part of the LinkedIn.com social network!

4. **YouTube.com and other video sites** – Videos continue in gaining popularity on an enormous scale. Google especially (*who incidentally owns YouTube*) loves to list video links in their search results. For you this could mean that if you have a popular video on YouTube.com and your video has the right SEO, it could potentially bring a huge stream of potential clients and interested parties to your video and website.

Blogging

Another way to gain more exposure for your freelance venture is creating blog posts for your website. If you have a WordPress based website, this is as easy as using a word processor and writing your post content.
WordPress also offers additional tools to make this process very easy and efficient. You will be able to add images to your post or include videos and with either free or paid for plugins you can add additional functionality to your website.

Once you have created your blog posts, you want to share this post with your intended audience through the channels in the previous section.

But before you do decide to share your posts, please ensure that they have quality content you are proud to share. This means that if only one person agrees that your post is worth sharing them in turn may share it with others, who then may share it with their contacts... You get the picture...

Another important aspect to consider when writing your blog posts is to make sure they are in line with your brand values and current to the market you are in. In essence your subject matters should be 'Hot'. Stay clear of making any controversial comments, political statements or anything that could be a 'bone of contention' to your audience.

If you want to go further you could always write about other major players in your niche, major brands that you want to be associated with. This in turn could be a win-win situation, since the major brand may want to comment or even link to your post, thereby increasing your audience even further.

This of course will only work if you are writing about them in a positive way, trashing them will have the exact opposite effect.

Once again, if you wish to make it easy for your website visitors to share your blog posts on Twitter, LinkedIn, Facebook or other social networking sites with the least amount of fuss, and your website is WordPress based, then there are numerous free Social Networking (Sharing) plugins to do this quickly and easily.

... Have you noticed by now, how much I love the simplicity of WordPress??...

How about then going the other way too? Instead of just writing blog posts for your own site, why not write content for other blogs too? Those blogs of course should not only be related to the niche you are working in and being in line with your expertise, but should also already have a much larger audience than your own site.

Get in touch with the blog site owner and enquire if he/she would be interested in having you as a guest blogger to provide content for their site in exchange for allowing you to link from your guest blog post content back to your own site.

While doing this it is important that it is a fresh post and not just a copy of a post that already exists on your own site. Not only would search engines not like this approach of copying content, but your audience on either site would feel cheated if they read one article on one site, only to find the same on your own. It just wouldn't give the professional image you are after and will potentially turn people away.

My wisecracking comment to this would be:
'It's like a paper cut which you don't notice at first, but as time goes on it starts to hurt...'

Personal Relationships & Associations

Even though we are so internet orientated these days, nothing beats personal interaction. Finding other people in your area to connect with at a professional level remains the best way to grow your connections.

If you look around, I am sure there are lots of events or even local networking groups which you could attend or join. These will allow you to meet likeminded people and business owners who share the same interests as you and will be interested in you and your brand.

Just use Google to search for business events in your city, maybe even adding the term 'professional' to your search. A website which comes to mind is MeetUp.com where other people and/or business owners organise events and invite others to attend. If you are really adventurous you could even launch your own MeetUp event.

Online Advertising

Even though we have touched on advertising previously, I want to spend a few more moments on the subject of online advertising. Advertising on the web is one of your best options to segment your advertising efforts, giving you lots of tools to address the best audience for your business.

Online advertising is also commonly referred to as PPC (**P**ay **P**er **C**lick) advertising, just to throw this in at this point.

Online advertising segmentation will allow you to not only place an advert, but to be specific of who the advert will be seen by, such as people in a specific region or country, a certain gender, a fine-tuned age-group and a whole lot more.

Here are my suggestions of online advertising options for you to explore:

1. **Google.com & other search engines** – Google advertising is done through their Google Adwords program. This is probably the largest PPC ad network on the planet with the largest audience you could ever want or even wish for.

   But their Adwords management dashboard does take some getting used to. Luckily though they have excellent support in place to help you, in case you get stuck. Create your advert, add the keywords which are important to your services and link the ad back to your website.

2. **FaceBook.com** – Starting at just about $1 per day, their advertising program allows you to not just place an ad, but to segment your target audience by

selecting age, gender, city, country and much more. This makes FaceBook.com probably the 2nd best choice of online advertising.

3. **LinkedIn.com** – As the only designated professional network in my online advertising options list, LinkedIn.com is THE one you must consider. Not only does it have very similar segmentation criteria options as the 2 previous ones, but it furthermore allows you to be even more professional, by including company size, audience level per sector etc.

Even though I mentioned it previously, don't forget to optimise your brand exposure by doing your Search Engine Optimisation (SEO), to assist Google to list your site in the best position within the search results. This in turn does apply to your adverts in just the same way.

Now that all the technical business stuff has been dealt with - Let's focus on running your freelance business!

How to & How much to charge for your services

Of course, in any business, the aspect is very much on being profitable. So even as a freelancer you do need to start thinking about yourself as a business. This takes us to the point of defining what to charge for your services.

By default, most freelancers do charge by the hour. But this may also depend on other factors, such as your local market, the type of services you provide, the type of job it is, etc.

Let me share with you some ideas to help you decide which way may best for you:

- Compare prices for similar work in your local area. This may give you an indication of what fees are classed as a common 'going rate', without over or even under charging for your own services.

- Work out what your annual costs are. Then doing your own maths, you can work out what your costs are per day, taking into account the days you do not work, plus any vacation time you wish to set for the year.

As a very basic example (*you can learn more about fee setting when searching on Google*):

Let's say my expenses are 10000 per year and I wish to earn 30000. Adding both together gives me a combined target total of 40000, which I need to earn – and to break even, ie. not leaving myself with a shortfall and unable to paying the rent or other costs.

If I then take 365 days in year, deduct my weekends and also my vacation time and public holidays, I may end up with around 225 actual working days.

To calculate the daily rate I would have to charge my clients to make those figures work in my favour, I will have to take the total value of the year 40000 and divide it by the number of actual working days, 225.

40000 : 225 = 177.77, rounded up to **180.00** per day

As I said, this is the most basic form to show you how fee setting can be done. To approach fee setting more professionally, there are free spreadsheets available for download to make this a more accurate approach. Search Google for 'free business budget templates'.

Remember that the above example is based on a break-even scenario. To add profit on top of your break-even figure, I would work on about 20-25% mark-up, which would take you to a daily fee of 225.00, without over or undercharging.

- In addition to the basic fee setting, other factors could be used to increase your fees further, such as the difficulty of the job or the time urgency of the client requirement. Rush jobs can demand a higher fee due to the urgency of delivering within a tight time-frame.

- You could also quote on a project as a whole. This may be great if you can foresee exactly the work involved and the time it will take you to complete the whole job. This is commonly known as 'estimating'.

It will require you to write a complete service delivery plan, outlining all tasks involved, time spend on those tasks and anything else relevant to the project.

While this approach may be very transparent for your client, it may hold potential pitfalls, which could cost **you** money and cut your profits, such as:

- You may have miscalculated the time it would take to complete the project.
- You may have missed important steps within the project and realised it only after the quote has been accepted.
- Your client may have missed important information about the project, for you to correctly estimate it.

Lastly there is the '*options*' approach you can give to your clients, for instance:

- Any clients you already 'own', such as past employers, friends or family members, your approach could be setting your fees within a low, medium or high price option.

    Just because you already know them though doesn't mean to do a lower quality job. Even though you may charge them slightly different rates, they still do expect the same quality of work as other clients.

- Any new clients you may get to work with may have a lot of expectations of what you can/should do for them.

    While I would not wish to turn down clients, it

always pays to give them options, such as breaking your services down into packages:

- **Option 1**: I will do A, B, C for x amount
- **Option 2**: I will do ABC & D & E for x amount
- **Option 3**: I will quote on your complete project, once we have agreed on the tasks you wish me to cover for you. (*If the client is happy with the quote, great, if not, you can then discuss shaving some aspects of the project and reduce the price and your workload that way*).

• You could potentially and initially lower your prices until you get more clients on board. While this is an option, you may find it harder later to increase your prices.

Furthermore some clients, even though they love saving money, may view your services at a lower quality than your competition (*even though it isn't*) and hire them instead of you...

Pricing your services can be somewhat of a tight-rope, never knowing which approach may work best for you and your various clients.

It would be worthwhile to decide on a standard pricing foundation on which your business will operate and then fine-tune it to the individual clients as you go along.

One really good first meeting question to ask is '**What is your budget for this project**'? This may indicate to you first off not just how much the client is willing to spend, but also highlights to you the importance of the project in monetary terms of investment. You can then adjust your fees accordingly.
If you think this may be a sneaky approach – 'Hey... Welcome to the world of business'!

Legal Stuff – Terms & Conditions, Privacy Policy etc.

As part of your website and your business as a whole, you should include documentation which explains your business Terms & Conditions as well as your Privacy Policy. These are also required by Google when reviewing your website for inclusion in their search engine listing.

In some countries it is even a legal requirement to display your real contact and business registration details on your business website.

Lastly I would like you to note that any Europe based websites are now required by law to display a 'Cookie' notice.

You can find tons of free Terms & Conditions and Privacy Policy document templates online, which you can amend to your own requirements.
If you want your Terms & Conditions to be more legally binding, it will be better to have these prepared by a qualified legal representative in order to protect yourself and your work.

Additional pages you may wish to consider to add are:

- Copyright statement
- Rights and responsibilities for both you and your clients
- Payment Terms
- Anything you feel important enough to add

Do not go overboard though as some clients may get turned off by your bureaucracy overload. It's also worth noting that most clients will have their own T&C's and Privacy Policy, which in many cases will supersede your own.

In addition to having your Terms & Conditions and other legal documents on your website, you should always supply a printed or PDF version for your clients to review, and sign where applicable, as part of your hiring contract.

You did realise that you should have a signed contract with any client you do work for, didn't you? I would never recommend undertaking any project work without having a signed contract, outlining all important aspects of the work undertaken, details of the project, such as parts to be completed, the time frame to be completed in and of course the agreed rate of remuneration.

A signed contract will aid you in supporting your claim against any client who may fail in paying you for your services.

Invoicing for your services

Depending on the agreement with your client, you may invoice once at the end of the whole project or on an interim or monthly basis. Some freelancers have been known to even take a 50% deposit at the time of signing the project assignment contract.

Payment options would, for simplicity, also need to be included in your Terms & Conditions statement.

Invoicing is the document which tells your client how much to pay you at this time. Depending on where you reside the details in the invoice may vary somewhat, especially the sales tax content. But usually they are very much alike in what details are being listed:

- Invoice date
- Service description
- Amount charged per transaction
- Required tax and legal details, such as VAT Number & VAT Rate
- Options of payment, such as Direct Bank Transfer, credit card, PayPal, cash, etc.

- Payment Due Date – usually set around 30 days Net after the invoice date. Sometime this can be as low as 14 days or as high as 90 days. The fewer days it is the better for you as you will get paid faster.

Clients – Your daily bread & butter

Now that you own a business and are your own brand, you are wholly responsible for your clients. They are the building block to your successful business and revenue and you cannot afford to lose them.

If you deliver consistent quality in your work and you exceed your client expectations, they will be very happy to be associated with your brand, recommend your brand to others and will be happy to return to you if need be.

Sadly, there may be times when you will be unable to retain customers. Maybe he/she has gone bust, or they are not willing to pay your fees... While this can and does happen, there is no need to panic just yet. Unless they are bankrupt of course, then there is no point in retaining them.

There is nothing stopping you though in doing some research on the financial state of any client before you sign a contract with them.

Some time ago I provided my training services for a well known training company here in the UK. Then, after they did not pay my invoice even after 2 reminders, I did some online research and discovered that they are in financial dire straits, showing debts of almost £200k, yet they were and still are trading!

Only after I threatened with court action, and almost 6 months after the actual invoice date, did they finally pay my outstanding bill. It goes without saying that I shall no longer do any more work for this client...

On a positive note though, most clients are very easy to retain as long as you are following some simple pointers. Your key-factor to retaining a brand-client relationship is to ensure that you are giving your clients that special attention while exceeding their expectations.

Before giving you more details on this going forward, here are 3 key factors you must maintain at all times (*in no particular order*):

1. Always deliver outstanding work
2. Always be highly professional
3. Always charge a fair price for your services

Let's see how we can break these down further:

Always deliver outstanding work

This goes without saying really. It is what any client will expect from you as the bare minimum. While this may vary from project to project, here are some tips on '**How to be GREAT**':

- **Always pay attention** – to what your client is saying. Maintaining your interest on what is being said will allow you to forge a much closer relationship with your client. Try to anticipate their needs and expectations. In line with those you will then be able to define your work more accurately. This will help you to pick up on their manners and habits and assist you in knowing how best to deliver your work as they want it.

- **Always plan ahead** – As the old saying goes "*Failing to plan is a plan to fail*". Always prepare your work and yourself in advance, trying to eliminate any last minute surprises where possible. The world is a nuthouse and sometimes things just get crazy; suddenly your client may need things you didn't know they would, or they suddenly want you to do something else you didn't know they may ask you for.

    By planning ahead, you can schedule some open time in your day or project to cover such unforeseen additions. Sometimes you may even be unable to follow your own plan due to unforeseen meetings or other events. Plan ahead as much as you can helps you to keep ahead while allowing you to have a contingency or fallback in place to stop you panic.

- **Over-deliver while getting better every time** – Clients love someone who gives them extra. Try to give them more than what is asked for or planned to be done.

Sometimes a project that at first seemed rather involved turns out to be easier and faster to deliver. This would allow you, without cutting corners or compromise on quality, to finish the project before the deadline. This would allow you to make a small adjustment on the fee if you so wish. Either way, the client will love you.

- **NEVER miss your deadline(s)** – This is the exact opposite to the point above. If you really want to agitate a client, then miss your deadline(s) and say goodbye to the relationship.

Since you may have had some involvement in setting the deadline(s) in the first place, nothing aggravates a client more than a broken promise.

- **You cannot do everything** – Get to know your own limits. Being able to multi-task is a great thing, but it isn't always easy. You will have to be honest of what you will be able to do in the time allotted. Taking on more than you can comfortably handle will get you in trouble.

  You will lose focus and have you running around like a headless chicken. Ultimately something will go wrong and the client will only see that fail. He/she will not be interested in excuses of 'I had so much to do... or If I had less things to do at once...'.

  This one failure to deliver could tarnish your brand reputation badly, since people usually remember bad things more than 10 good ones.

Exceeding expectations

This sounds wonderful, doesn't it? We all like to receive a little more than what we have to pay for. You will quickly come to realise that some clients will not care much for that exceeded expectations stuff or even come to realise it. But then again, who told you that life was fair...?

But some of them do – and if they do, they praise you to everyone they know, scoring you BIG points on their Richter scale.

To help you to score those big points, you need to try to understand what others, before you, may have failed in doing and avoid making the same mistakes. Here are some more tips:

- **Make them feel important** – Show interest in what your clients are working on, getting their opinions on the work they want you to do or any work you have done for them previously. Once you have their opinions or suggestions, try to incorporate them into your work.

- **Add more value than what they asked for** – Have a good think about what additional extras you could give your clients.

    Given your expertise on the project you are working on you could share tips and tricks of how to get the best out of the system or software, if this is your field. Alternatively you may want to share with them support materials in relation to the project, which in turn may help them in some way.

    It's hard for me to suggest exact ideas since I don't know what market your business operates in, but I am sure that some soul searching will give you ideas of what value you could offer.

But you need to be careful, that any additional value you offer does not become an expectation and let's clients get used to it. If you always offer any value additions, sooner or later your client will no longer see it as a favour, but expects this as part of your standard service delivery.

- **Feel proud to be associated with their company** – It takes time to build a brand-client relationship. By always talking about your clients in glorious colour with other people, let them know about it. Always show them that you appreciate their business. Some freelancers may send holiday cards to their clients, I don't.

Other things to do to keep in good stead with your clients

- **Always return their calls in good time** – Nothing is more annoying than waiting for someone to reply to a message left on a machine. Don't delay…!

- **Always be flexible** – Adapt to the client's needs and/or demands. Don't come across as picky, enquire what they may need and if needed, how they would like you to do it.

- **Staying in contact with the client** – Once a project has finished, you may not hear from them again for quite some time, if at all… Make the first move and touch base with them again. Drop them an email to enquire how they are getting on or if there is anything else you may be able to help them with.

   Even though it may feel great that they don't bother you, the importance here is to ensure that they don't forget about you and your excellent services.

- **Keep it personal** – without overdoing it!
    - Greet them when you see them
    - Ask how things are going
    - Ask how they are doing
    - Make small talk

- Grow a closer bond between both of you
- **Show respect and talk the way they do** – Always adjust yourself to the way they talk and/or they way they address each other. Be respectful in your approach. Everyone is different and it is imperative that you try to fit in.

Things which surely will kill your client relationship

The following list is a collection of absolute "*No No's*", to be avoided at all cost:

- **Denying your mistakes** – We are all making mistakes, even you. That's life. And if the unfortunate happens, don't deny your mistakes, don't blame others and for goodness sake – don't make excuses!

- **Raising invoices without the clients' approval** – This will sure-fire you to the land of never-never land. While estimating your project fees and costs always leave room for contingency extras and let the client know about it.

  Charging for something the client did not know will be costing extra will certainly cause trouble and lose you any future work, if not being kicked off the project right there.

- **Removing any property from the client site** – No matter how small or insignificant it may appear to you, taking anything without permission can get you reported to the police for theft.

Needless to say, you will never work for that or their associates ever again.

Quite a few years ago, I was working with other freelancers on a huge international project assignment for a major corporate client. One Friday afternoon I left the site like any other day. The following Monday, one of the freelancers didn't turn up for work.

On enquiring of his whereabouts with the client, I was informed that on the Friday he was caught, during a security check, removing 2 reams of printing paper from the office without permission. He was immediately fired from the project and was never mentioned by the client thereafter, nor have I ever heard of or seen him since...

Now that you have come to the end of this book, all I can say is that I wish you all the very best in your freelance career.

It certainly can be one of the best steps you take in your life, as long as you are fully committed to your own success.

There are millions of us out there, so welcome to the club!

Resources

Here are some links to websites that may come in handy as a freelancer:

Freelancer Portals

- Upwork (*formerly ODesk*) – www.odesk.com
- TopTotal – www.toptotal.com
- eLance – www.elance.com
- Freelancer – www.freelancer.com
- Craigslist – www.craigslist.com
- GuRu – www.guru.com
- 99 Designs – www.99designs.com
- People-per-Hour – www.peopleperhour.com
- Freelance Writing Gigs – freelancewritinggigs.com
- Demand Media – www.demandmedia.com
- College Recruiter – www.collegerecruiter.com
- Get-a-Coder – www.getacoder.com
- iFreelance – www.ifreelance.com
- Project4Hire – www.project4hire.com
- SimplyHired – www.simplyhired.com
- Envato Studio – www.studio.envato.com
- Fiverr – www.fiverr.com

- Dribble – www.dribble.com/jobs/
- Behance Job – www.behance.net/joblist/
- WordPress – www.jobs.wordpress.net
- LinkedIn – www.linkedin.com/job/
- Smashing Jobs – www.jobs.smashingmagazine.com
- Krop – www.krop.com
- MeFi Jobs – www.jobs.metafilter.com
- Coroflot – www.coroflot.com/jobs/
- Problogger Jobs – www.jobs.problogger.net
- Dice – www.dice.com
- WPHired – www.wphired.com
- We work Remotely – www.weworkremotely.com
- Hirable – www.wearehireable.com
- Crew – www.crew.co
- Gun.io – www.gun.io
- LocalSolo – www.localsolo.com
- OnSite – www.onsite.io
- Folyo – www.folyo.me
- Gigster – www.trygigster.com
- HireMyFriend – www.hiremyfriend.io
- YunoJuno – www.yunojuno.com
- Crowdsite – www.crowdsite.com
- Joomlancers – www.joomlancers.com
- JavaScript Ninja Jobs – www.jobs.jsninja.com
- GigScribe – www.gigscribe.com
- LocaLancers – www.localancers.com
- SoloGig – www.sologig.com
- Authentic Jobs – www.authenticjobs.com

- CrowdSPRING – www.crowdspring.com
- DesignCrowd – www.designcrowd.com
- Working Nomads – www.workingnomads.co
- Bark – www.bark.com
- Matchist – www.matchist.com
- CampusJob – www.campusjob.com
- AirPair – www.airpair.com
- Traction – www.gotraction.com
- Juiiicy – www.juiiicy.com

Accounting Software

- WaveApps – www.waveapps.com
- BeanBalance – www.beanbalance.com
- BrightBook – www.mybrightbook.com
- Pandle – www.mypandle.co.uk
- Accounter – www.accounterlive.com
- KashFlow – www.kashflow.com

Free Office Software

- SoftMaker FreeOffice – www.freeoffice.com
- LibreOffice – www.libreoffice.org
- Apache Open Office – www.openoffice.org

Social Networks

- Twitter – www.twitter.com
- Facebook – www.facebook.com
- LinkedIn – www.linkedin.com
- Google+ – www.plus.google.com
- YouTube – www.youtube.com
- Pintrest – www.pintrest.com
- Instagram – www.instagram.com
- Tumblr – www.tumblr.com
- Flickr – www.flickr.com
- Reddit – www.reddit.com
- Quora – www.quora.com
- Vine – www.vine.co
- BizSugar – www.bizsugar.com
- StumbleUpon – www.stumbleupon.com
- Digg – www.digg.com

Domain Name & Hosting Services

- Hostgator – www.hostgator.com
- GoDaddy – www.godaddy.com
- A2Hosting – www.a2hosting.com
- SiteGround – www.siteground.com
- DreamHost – www.dreamhost.com

Other books by the author

Now available on Amazon worldwide:

Don't Stress – Relax, ISBN: 978-1502911070

Build a high income business as a Professional Speaker, ISBN: 978-1493740345

How to grow your therapy business, ASIN: B0078FY89E

7 Secrets to Create Attractiveness with your Body Language, ASIN: B00AFKTIC6

www.ingramcontent.com/pod-product-compliance
Lightning Source LLC
Chambersburg PA
CBHW071824200526
45169CB00018B/990